MUCH CRY

OF

KENDAL WOOL

An Anthology (?1420-1720)

Compiled with an introduction by

the late Edward M. Wilson, M.A., Ph.D., F.B.A.

Curwen Archives Trust,
County Record Office,
Kendal

TO THE MEMORY

OF

Donald F. Curwen,

whose friendship I valued.

ACKNOWLEDGEMENTS

I must thank Dr. D. S. Brewer, F.S.A., Master of Emmanuel College, for help with the attribution to Lydgate of my extract no. 1. Professor G. R. Elton, F.B.A., kindly enlightened me about the authorship of no. 5; I disregarded his advice about using the edition of 1969 as I preferred to quote the one available to Sir Thomas Smith's early readers. For nos. 9 and 10 I am grateful to the Secretary and Council of the Malone Society for their permission to quote from their editions of the two plays of *Robert Earl of Huntington*; to the Scolar Press for theirs to quote from the reprint of the fourth edition of *Thomas of Reading* (no. 14) which I have verified against the copy in the British Library; to E. A. Horsman and to the Liverpool University Press for their permission to use the 1956 reprint of the edition of 1632 of *The Pinder of Wakefield*; and for No. 26 to Mr. Christopher Morris (of King's College, Cambridge) and the Cresset Press for their permission to reprint from their edition of Celia Fiennes's *The Journeys* of 1947. To Mr. J. C. T. Oates, F.B.A., I owe my acquaintance with Ralph Tyrer's *Five Godlie Sermons*; I thank him too.

Song of three Parts

For Folded Flocks, on Fruitful Plains,
The Shepherds and the Farmers Gains,
    Fair Britain *all the World outvyes;*
And Pan, *as in* Arcadia *Reigns,*
    Where Pleasure mixt with Profit lyes.

Though Jasons *Office was Famed of old,*
The British *Wool is growing Gold;*
    No mines can more of Wealth supply:
It keeps the Peasant from the Cold,
    And takes for Kings the Tyrian *Dye.*

John Dryden, *King Arthur: Or, The British Worthy,* London 1695, p. 38. The opera –
with music by Henry Purcell – was performed in December, 1691.

CONTENTS

INTRODUCTION

I hope that this anthology can stand on its own feet. Its main intention is to give an idea of the publicly held reputation of the Kendal wool-trade before 1720. The following extracts were, with a few exceptions, printed before that date; the exceptions were written to inform other people and perhaps put in a form ready to be printed (nos. 2, 24, 25, 26). The selection is also intended to supplement, illustrate or contrast with already published accounts chiefly derived from record offices. On the whole they bear some relation to the pages on Kendal wool contained in Canon C. M. L. Bouch's and Professor G. P. Jones's *A Short Economic History of the Lake Counties 1500-1830* (Manchester University Press, 1961, pp. 132-7, 140-1), in which the authors quoted shorter fragments from my nos. 15 and 17. My debt to their investigations will be obvious to those who read that interesting book. Mr. M. Davies-Shiel in his monograph *Wool is my bread* (Kendal, 1975) quoted portions of my nos. 1, 7 and 19; his work on the use of lye-pits in the preparation of local wool seems to me commendable, but I differ from him when he discusses in his pamphlet some historical matters. Mr. Bruce C. Jones's 'Westmorland Pack-horse Men in Southampton' (CW2, LIX (1959), 65-84) – a brilliant study of Kendal's exports – receives unexpected confirmation in my no. 9 and some picturesque, not strictly historical, background from nos. 15, 18 and 21.

Though this anthology includes extracts from a few works that can be counted as literature (e.g. nos. 7, 8, 14), any merit it possesses as a whole is illustrative of social and economic history. It cannot claim completeness, but a fairly long search preceded its publication. The first item is a ham-fisted description of Bacchus from a poem attributed to John Lydgate by William Caxton's successor Wynkyn de Worde in 1498; the attribution is not accepted by modern scholars, and the poem cannot be proved to be earlier than 1463. The god is said to carry on his head a jolly crown of vine-leaves, a threadbare Kendal hood, a gimlet and a faucet! The anonymous author can have had little visual imagination to resort to such diverse objects, but he felt compelled so to arrange them as symbols of drunkenness and improvidence. The point is that Kendal cloth was cheap, and the god of wine had almost worn it out.

John Leland (1506-1552) was an early English antiquary, who had probably visited Kendal. His descriptions of both the town and its trade (no. 2) probably lie behind those of William Camden (1551-1623) in his Latin *Britannia* (no. 6) and its English translation by Philemon Holland (no. 12). Notice the similarity between Leland's

Emporium laneis pannis celeberrimum

and Camden's

Lanificij gloria et industria ita praecellens . . . .

Camden's praises of the wool industry were more verbose ('very great trade and resort . . . excellent clothing . . . industrie so surpas-sing . . . a great name . . . great trafficke and vent of their woollen clothes throughout England'), and they are echoed – along with his remark about Kendal's 'two broad and long streets crossing the one over the other', in several later items (nos. 16, 20, 21, 24, 25). All these passages stress the importance of the trade in itself, and, without disguising that it was concerned with cheap cloth, they stress its social effects and its wide range throughout the country. Mr. Bruce Jones's article proves that this was no empty statement; Bouch and Jones support him.

Outlaws

Early ballads about Robin Hood dress him and his men in 'Lincoln green' (see notes to no. 3), but the anonymous *Playe of Robyn Hoode* (no. 3) of 1560 or earlier gives them Kendal green to wear. (A sign, perhaps that the Kendal trade had then exceeded that of Lincoln?) The Friar describes Robin's men as 'ragged knaues . . . Clothed all in Kendale greene', but after his fight with Robin, the Friar joins his company. In Anthony Munday's two plays about *Robert Earl of Huntington* (nos. 9 and 10) – *alias* Robin Hood, the same example is followed. In *scena ix* of *The Downfall* Scarlet tells how 'Bateman of Kendall gaue vs Kendall greene'; in *scena xii* Prince John decides to disguise himself, like the outlaws, in the same cloth; and in *scena xv* the Prince compares himself with the Pinder of Wakefield and quotes a verse from an earlier text of the Ballad of Robin Hood and that Pinder:

> At Michaelmas commeth my couenant out,
>   My master giues me my fee:
> Then *Robin* Ile weare thy Kendall greene,
>   And wend to the greenewodde with thee.

In *The death of Robert Earl of Huntington* the Friar tells the men to doff their 'Kendall greene' and put on mourning for Robin's Matilda, 'his

2

fair maid Marian'. The Pinder of Wakefield does not appear in either play, but besides the Prince, Scarlet mentioned both George a Greene of Bradford and 'wanton Wakefields Pinner'; we shall meet the latter again in no. 15, and the two are identified in no. 18. More important though, is Scarlet's mention of 'Bateman of Kendall'; Mr. Bruce Jones tells us of eleven different Batemans from Kendal who visited Southampton between 1492 and 1576. May not Munday's reference be to a remembered Kendal chapman known to some members of his audience?

If Robin Hood's men were thought to have worn Kendal green, the same clothing could well have suited the misbegotten knaves of Falstaff's fantasy (no. 7). *Henry IV, part I* was printed before Munday's two Robin Hood plays, but that does not necessarily prove that Shakespeare's play was written earlier than either of Munday's.

A Husbandman, Serving Men, a Ploughman and a Mayor

If Kendal cloth was suitable for men who ran wild in Sherwood Forest, it would also protect those who worked on the land or did other manual labour. In an anonymous mid-sixteenth century verse debate between Pride and Lowliness we are shown a fifty-year-old man who kept his place, was softly spoken, had a face burned by the sun and seemed to portray sincerity and truth. He was a husbandman and wore a coat of very coarse Kendal cloth (no. 4). The anonymous author drew a more consistent portrait than that contained in our no. 1. Here the rough Kendal clothes are typical of a man who is honest, hard-working, unassuming and sincere: a sixteenth century Piers Plowman.

Sir Thomas Smith (1513-77) was a scholar, statesman and political theorist. His *Discourse of the Commonwealth of this realm of England*, composed apparently in 1549, was printed posthumously in 1581 and was often reprinted. Our extract (no. 5) does not represent the full scope of this treatise which is so important for political historians. The husbandman in no. 4 makes a contrast with the serving man described here, though the feeling that lies behind both extracts is the traditional one. The wealthy and noble were entitled to wear good cloth; the humble must content themselves with poorer stuff. So Smith's serving man despises his 'Kendall coate' and desires one of 'the finest cloth maie be had for money', as he also hankers after more elaborate food and breeches expensively dyed. Such men are regarded by the uncertain author as a sign of decadence, and they involve their masters in

3

unnecessary expense. (The author does not mention that the masters themselves possibly prided themselves on the fine liveries their men wore to outdo those provided by their neighbours.)

The ploughman (no. 8) described by Joseph Hall (1574-1656) seems to me one of the best-written pieces in this collection. The ploughman envies a soldier's fine clothes and Indian loot, scorning his own workaday clothes of 'Kendall-greene'. Though before he had been happy enough to go whistling to his work, he now sells his team and enlists. Hall gives in a brief couplet a summary of the horrors of war; the ploughman has by far the happier life. (Hall was born a country boy.) In these three extracts Kendal cloth is made to accompany a sense of decent social order, the dignity of labour and peace rather than the flashy horrors of soldiering, or pride and extravagance near home.

I know nothing about Robert Richmond except that he contributed – along with many other poets – mock-laudatory poems to Tom Coryat's *Crudities,* a garrulous account of the author's travels in Europe, printed in 1611. Richmond relates (no.13) how Henry VIII was to visit Hartlepool, and the Mayor and his Council met to consider how best to welcome that monarch. One member suggested they give him a skate-fish, but the Mayor thought that too little, let the king have one and a half! As the Mayor overdid the present, so Coryat related not more than the truth but certainly more than other travellers told. The story is mildly funny, but the application to Coryat is lame and far-fetched. We need note only that after the three items just mentioned the 'Kendall gowne' helps to make the Mayor an object of ridicule. I suspect that Richmond must have been a Londoner.

Kendal breeches are used also to a ridiculous purpose in the parody of Virgil's *Aeneid IV* (no. 22) by Charles Cotton, the collaborator of Isaac Walton in *The Compleat Angler.* The result is tasteless. The point seems to be that a hero is burlesqued by wearing a plebeian garment.

Kendal Cottons from inside Kendal

Queen Mary I gave the advowson of Kendal Parish Church to Trinity College, Cambridge. In 1575 Queen Elizabeth I granted a charter to Kendal, which provided for its government by an Alderman and twenty-four councillors. (There was no mayor of Kendal until the charter of Charles I, granted in 1637). Ralph Tyrer, B.D., a former scholar of Westminster School and a fellow of Trinity College, was appointed vicar of Kendal in 1592 and remained there until his death in

1626. In 1602 he dedicated his *Fiue Godlie Sermons* to the Alderman, Senior Burgess and other members of the Kendal Corporation. In this dedication he referred to the prosperity that the Charter had brought to the town (no longer a country village) and to God's goodness in letting Trinity College provide their parish priests (no. 11). Although he refers somewhat slightingly to the 'meane yet necessarie commodities' (i.e. Kendal cottons) produced there, he testifies that Kendal has now become as rich as Tyre (there is, I think, an implicit pun on his own surname). Would that the town could become equally famous for its 'fruitfull obedience to the word' and 'feruent zeale'. The testimony of this cultured parson, in Kendal, but not of it, is evidence of the town's prosperity in the early years of the seventeenth century. (A paper entitled 'Ralph Tyrer, Vicar of Kendal – 1592 to 1627 appeared in CW2 recently.)

Richard Brathwait (or Brathwaite) was born at Burneside Hall, Strickland Roger (near Kendal), probably in 1588. He may have learned the classical languages from Ralph Tyrer; afterwards he studied at Oriel College, Oxford and at the Inns of Court. He returned to the North West after some relatively profitless years in London, and in 1617 he married a Yorkshire woman. The births of his children are entered in the Kendal registers. Frances Brathwait, his first wife, died in 1635; four years later he married Mary Crofts of Kirtlington, Yorkshire, which brought him the manor of Catterick, where he mainly resided until his death at East Appleton in 1673. He supported the royal cause in the Civil War and was heavily fined as a consequence.

He wrote and published voluminously between 1611 and 1665. There are more extracts from his works in this anthology than from those of any other writer; no less than five separate extracts, printed from 1615 to 1665, throw light on the Kendal wool trade. He wrote on many subjects: religious poetry and prose, secular poetry, popular history, satire, convivial prose and poetry, characters, tales and novels, courtesy books, a commentary on Chaucer's Miller's and Wife of Bath's tales, etc. Unfortunately his prose is often careless and prolix; his verse has much the same qualities. Only his humorous works, such as the Latin macaronics of *Barnabees Journall* and the English prose of *Ar't asleepe, Husband? A boulster lecture* are tolerable to the cultivated reader.

In 1615 he published a collection of verse satires called *A Strappado for the Diuell*; in it are several poems concerned with Kendal, but only one deals with the wool trade. It has a more elaborate title but it is usually referred to as *To the Cottoneers of Kendal*. It is 612 lines long, but I have reprinted only 202 (no. 15). Bouch and Jones quoted 13 lines or fragments of lines from it; I think that a more generous sample tells more even than they did. The verses are often clumsy and occasionally obscure, but he meant what he said most of the time. His social superiority to the wool men he addressed enabled him to speak the truth in love to them. His praises seem to me to be sincere, and his criticisms are strong. I must therefore ask my readers to put aside prejudices against didactic verse and to read carefully the sections of the poem which I have here selected, tedious though they may be.

I have numbered the lines in this poem so that the reader may see the length of the omitted passages. At the beginning he praises the way in which linings of Kendal cottons compensate the bodily defects of Irish serving men. Man does not appear a true man unless he is substantially dressed! Then he divides his address into three parts: (i) The social benefit of the trade to the poor; (ii) The trade enriches Englishmen, not foreigners; (iii) He will prove that it derives from antiquity.

(i) Wool work supports the children of the poor, who can from their earliest years complete such light work as winding spools and other tasks. Brathwait urges the cottoneers not to delay their due payment to the poor families who carry out such work. If the factors delay paying the chapmen who in turn put off paying the workers, a sin has been committed which cries to heaven for vengeance (see Matthew, 25. 41). The writer's social conscience leads him to invoke a religious punishment on those who keep poor men waiting for their wages. The penalty will presumably afflict the chapmen as well as the factors (lines 89-188).

(ii) The business is no monopoly or privilege. He praises the chapmen whose integrity shames those who are well dressed in silken clothes. He then reproves the shearmen who are apt to stretch the cloth unduly on their tenters (see Bouch and Jones, p. 135). He tells also of a 'Gallant in this towne' who bought thirty yards of rug to make a suit and cloak, which shrank to fifteen yards in the tailor's hands. Either the tailor was a thief, or 'The rugge was tentered more than did befit' (lines 203-54). (See also the remark made by Thomas Cole of Reading in the Deloney extract – no. 14 – and the quotation from Dekker's and Webster's *West-ward Hoe* in a note to it.)

(iii) The story of how Carmentis brought wool work to Kendal is a tiresome example of Brathwait's sham mythology. I quote, nevertheless, lines 357-70 because of the remarks about Staveley-in-Kendal, in spite of the appalling pun they contain. Was Staveley a centre of the trade, second only to Kendal? Or did he introduce the place simply because of its nearness to Burneside Hall?

The remainder of the poem is not entirely without interest. Brathwait's reference to the connections of Kendal tradesmen with Stourbridge fair near Cambridge (once one of the most famous fairs in England) is the first printed one I have come across. It precedes Thomas Fuller's account (see no. 21) but there is probably earlier manuscript material in the Cambridge University archives (lines 374-85). Again I must apologise for what must be Brathwait's worst pun in this passage.

There follows a passage about the 'white coats' of Kendal, interrupted by praises of the town irrelevant to our immediate subject. In the *New* (or *Oxford*) *English Dictionary* the white coats are defined as: Soldiers 'wearing a white or light-coloured coat', obsolete, except in a historical sense. According to Brathwait they were the local archers who defended the Border against the Scots. They rivalled in marksmanship the warriors of Scythia, Persia and Greece. Their name came from their home-spun clothes. Their enemies were so much terrified by them as to produce a physical reaction that I do not need to explain (lines 470-4, 529-36).

The concluding lines (537-612) recapitulate much that has gone before, mention the simple pleasures of the Kendalians and praise a citizen whose name he does not give.

The second extract from Brathwait's works (no. 17) was printed fifteen years after *The Strappado*. In this prose piece he repeated with greater clarity some of the points made about child-labour in the earlier work. Wool work is light, suitable for poor children; the family as a whole can collaborate in it; 'our late gracious sovereign' (presumably James I) freed this trade from taxation. Now, however, the trade is in distress; workmen – presumably weavers – cannot make ends meet. Government help is rumoured; when it comes the victims of the slump will be relieved to the greater glory of God and to the renown of His Majesty King Charles I. Bouch and Jones quoted some lines of this passage and added that there had been a severe depression in the wool trade between 1620 and 1625, and a shorter one in 1630. They hint too at a period of industrial distress in the North West during the thirties which possibly continued into the forties.

Brathwait's work *The Fatall Nuptiall*, printed in 1636 is poem with a prose preface about the accident to the Windermere ferry in 1635 in which over forty men and women perished (no. 19). Among them

7

were some Kendal shearmen, whose loss the author mourned. The lament includes a few lines about that 'useful mystery' which may puzzle modern readers. The shearmen made coarse cloth, which took no *alnage,* was useful to the Common-weal and was 'Fit for Sale, although unfit for Seale'. Bouch and Jones (p. 135) explained that poor northern cloth was, in 1390, exempted from conforming to regulations about fixed dimensions, and in 1407 and 1410 the vendors were excused the official sealing of such cloth. The duty on superior cloth was called alnage (because it was measured by the ell or yard). Difficulties about these regulations arose in 1597 through excessive tentering, and in 1601 justices examined the situation in three northern counties (including Westmorland). In 1609 a statute declared that the act of 1597 did not apply to 'Kendals and other coarse things of like nature and made of the like wool'. Brathwait's words here suggest that Charles I had approved the old exemptions. Sympathy for the poor workman is again obvious in these few lines of verse.

Brathwait's fourth extract (no. 20) is from the macaronic work already mentioned, *Barnabees Journall* or *Barnabae Itinerarium,* printed pseudonymously in 1638, rechristened *Drunken Barnaby's Four Journeys to the North of England* in 1717 and other later editions. The six-line stanza is the last in the third journey, and in it Kendal is described as governed by an Alderman; it must therefore have been composed before 1637, the date of Charles I's charter. The reference earlier to Nesham, the birth-place of his first wife, inclines me to think that he wrote it before his first marriage. The original footnotes quote the Kendal motto *Pannus mihi panis,* an extract from Camden's description of the town (nos. 6 & 12) and a distich about Kendal's government by a mayor – clearly added to the older text just before it went to press. I include this piece for the sake of completeness.

The fifth and last Brathwait extract is from an essay called *The interest of Westmerland* (no. 23), which I hope to publish in full elsewhere. It was written after the Restoration, when Brathwait was living at Catterick, and was printed in 1665. It deals mainly with the political situation in the county during and after the Civil Wars. I think that Brathwait revisited his old home, possibly during the composition of the essay, and that we can consider it as first-hand information. Kendal wool trade is still in need of help from the Government, he tells us; let us hope that 'that sharp *Northern ayr*' will blow away the self-interest of the elected representatives in Parliament.

In spite of Richard Brathwait's defects as a writer, his information about the Kendal wool-trade seems to me reliable, learned at first hand.

8

Kendal Wool Men in London and in the Provinces

Thomas Deloney's *Thomas of Reading* is an amusing account of the adventures in London of nine wool merchants. The earliest edition to survive is the fourth of 1612; the first three were probably read to pieces by contemporary purchasers of them. The full title contains the words *The sixe worthy yeomen of the West,* and the fourth edition is said to be 'corrected and enlarged by T.D.'. Presumably the three northern merchants '*Cutbert* of Kendall, *Hodgekins* of Hallifax, and *Martin Byram* of Manchester' and their doings were added in as part of the enlargements. I have extracted the passages which refer to Cuthbert as a wool man in my no. 14; his other adventures, brought about by his love affair with the London inn-keeper's wife, are most entertaining, but they are irrelevant to my present purpose. This early novel is unjustly neglected, although the fifth edition was reprinted in the first volume of *Shorter English Novels* in the Everyman Library. I ought to add that Cuthbert of Kendal appears to be a purely fictional character; his name does not appear either in Mr. Bruce Jones's article or in the Kendal *Boke of Recorde.*

The story is supposedly set in the reign of Henry I, but there is no attempt to recreate a historical background to the events described. We are told of the nine men's adventures in London lodgings and inns of the reign of Elizabeth I or that of James I. The language is straightforward, spiced with proverbial sayings and country set phrases. We hear of the country weavers' competition with Londoners and finally of the good they did in their home towns. Cuthbert, we are told, married twenty-three couples from his own house and gave each of them ten pounds 'to beginne the world withall'. He is at bottom a worthy man, and his peccadillos are amusing, punished and forgotten. A sly remark by old Thomas Cole of Reading about the shrinking of northern cloth reflects not only on Cuthbert but also on the merchants from Manchester and Halifax. The introductory paragraphs about child labour parallel Brathwait's in nos. 15 and 17. The whole work enables us to recreate the contemporary life implicit in Mr. Bruce Jones's records from the Southampton archives.

Cuthbert's men, if not Cuthbert himself, reappear in a chap-book devoted to George a-Green, now established as the Pinder of Wakefield, printed in 1632. The anonymous author of it has borrowed the names of the two wealthy yeomen '*Cuthbert* of *Kendall* and *Hoskins* [Hodgekins in Deloney] of *Hallifax*' from *Thomas of Reading.* The incidents described are fights between their 'lusty waine-men' and the

9

followers of George a-Green in Wakefield. A couple of affrays are related (I have contented myself with a summary of the first) in which the Kendalians and those of Halifax are made to submit to the humiliating conditions imposed by the Pinder on outsiders. After this, the victors and the vanquished together 'did liquor their insides as well they had their outsides basted' and parted with the promise to meet to fight again on Midsummer Day. This is a coarse, plebeian piece, without the charm of Deloney's narrative. Presumably such battles took place from time to time in the provinces; he would be a rash man who supposed that Kendal waggoners never had to defend themselves when they travelled in Yorkshire.

Stourbridge was once one of the great fairs held in England. It took place on Stourbridge common to the east of Cambridge and lasted well into this century. We have already seen how Richard Brathwait in his poem *To the Cottoneers* (no. 15, lines 374-85) referred to its Kendalian origin. This was confirmed by Thomas Fuller (1608-1661), a more reliable historian. His account, based on the records of the University of Cambridge, was printed in his history of that University (no. 21), printed in 1658. The whole story of the relation of Kendal cottons to this great fair needs further investigation. There seems to be no doubt that Kendal men took a part in it during many years of its existence.

This brings my survey to an end. I hope that I have pointed to the most interesting features of the extracts printed below. Perhaps there is one thing that I ought to add. I have seen no evidence whatever to prove that good-quality cloth was produced in Kendal during the period I have chosen. I do not accept the supposed present of suit lengths to Henry VIII and his jester from Queen Catherine Parr. No authority is quoted for this alleged gift, and it smacks more of twentieth century historical fantasy than of an authentic record. More possible is an item in the accounts of the Lady Anne Clifford, Countess of Dorset, Pembroke and Montgomery; on 18 August, 1673 she paid Mr. George Sedgwicke three pounds nineteen shillings and nine pence 'for 2: yards and 3: quarters of fine Scarlett Cloth at 29s. per yard which he bought for me at Kendall to give away'. (George C. Williamson, *Lady Anne Clifford,* Kendal, 1922, p. 508). It seems more probable that this expensive material was imported into Kendal than that it was manufactured there. To return finally to John Dryden's three-part song quoted at the beginning of this work, Kendal wool took no Tyrian dye for kings, but it preserved thousands of peasants from the cold; the descendants of spinners, weavers, fullers, shearman-dyers and chapmen can still be proud of this service of their ancestors to society.

A note on old spelling etc.

I have not modernised the spelling or the punctuation of the originals, although I have expanded occasional abbreviations. Those unaccustomed to the old conventions should remember that *i* and *j* were often interchangeable, as were *i* and *y*. *u* and *v* could be either consonants (modern *v*) or vowels (modern *u*). Their use depended on the position of the letter in the word; *v* was originally used as the first letter in the word (*very, vs, vnto, vpon,* etc.) whereas *u* was used as a letter after the first (*ouer, much, liue, driue*). The apostrophe before or after an *s* at the end of a word to denote possession (a genitive) was not used in any extract here printed (*Troys combustion* in no. 22; *the Taylors yard* and *Trades Antiquity* in no. 15). I have retained such uses for two reasons: (1) out of respect for the original authors and their printers; (2) because archaic spelling makes modern readers study those words more slowly and carefully. I hope that I have explained most of the 'hard words' in the final glossary.

1   [Bacchus]   *c.* 1465

Then came the good Bachus, and by her [Minerva] set hym downe,
  Holdyng in hys hande a cup full of wyne.
Of grene vyne leues he weryd a ioly crosne.   Bacchus sits by
  He was clad in clustres of grapes good and fyne.   her, clad in grape
  A garland of yuy he chase for his sygne;   clusters, a cup of
    On hys hede he had a thredebare kendall hood; wine in his hand.
  A gymlet and a fauset therupon stood.   His sign is a gar-
                                      land of yew.

John Lydgate [sic], *The Assembly of gods: or the Accord of Reason and Sensuality in the fear of Death* [?1420] [sic], ed. Oscar Lovell Triggs, Early English Text Society, Extra Series, LXIX, London, 1896, lines 351-7.
Notes. The attribution to Lydgate was disproved by Henry Noble MacCracken in *The Lydgate Canon* (Appendix to the Philological Society's Transactions, 1907-9), London, 1908, p. xxxii. See also Walter F. Schirmer, *John Lydgate,* London, 1961, pp. 275, 277; Derek Pearsall, *John Lydgate,* London, 1970, p. 60.
  The writer of the marginal annotations misread 'yuy' to mean 'yew'; but ivy was the plant sacred to Bacchus (see II Maccabees, vi. 7).

2   [Kendal]   Between 1534 and 1543

    In *Westmerland* is but one good Market Towne cawlled *Kendale,* otherwise, as I wene, *Kirkby Kendale.* Yt hath the name of the River cawlled *Kent, unde &* Kendale, *sed Emporium laneis pannis celeberrimum.* In the Towne is but one Chirch. The Circuite of the Paroch by the Cuntery adjacent hath many Chapels, and divers yn the Towne self. About half a Myle of on the East Side of the Town is on a Hil a Parke longging to yowng M. *Par,* the chyfest of that Name, and ther is a Place as it were a Castell.
    Kent* Ryver is of a good Depthe not wel to be occupied with Botes for rowllyng Stones and other Moles. Yt risith of very many Heddes, be lykelyhood springging withyn the same Shire.

  * A vii. or viii. Myles fro *Kentdale,* wher is a Mere communely cawllid *Kenmore* [sic].

  The Itinerary of John Leland the Antiquary, ed. by Thomas Hearne, third edition, Oxford, 1769, VII, 51-2.

3   1560

[Robin Hood and the Friar]

Fryer [Tucke]	Why wylt thou fyght a plucke
Robyn Hode	and God send me good lucke
Fryer	Than haue a stroke for fryer tucke
Robyn Hode	Holde thy hande frere and here me speke
Fryer	Saye on ragged knaue
	me seemeth ye begyn to swete
Robyn Hode	In this forest I haue a hounde
	I wyl not giue him for an hundredth pound
	Geue me leue my horne to blowe,
	That my hounde may knowe
Fryer	Blowe on ragged knaue without any doubte
	Vntyll bothe thyne eyes starte out
	Here be a sorte of ragged knaues come in
	Clothed all in kendale grene
	And to the they take their way nowe
Robyn Hode	Peraduenture they do so
Fryer	I gaue the leue to blowe at thy wyll
	Now giue me leue to whistell my fyll
Robyn Hode	Whystell frere euyl mote thou fare
	Vntyll bothe thyne eyes starte
Fryer	Now cut and bause
	Breng forth the clubbes and staues
	And downe with those ragged knaues
Robyn Hode	How sayest thou frere wylt thou be my man
	To do me the best servyse thou can
	Thou shal haue both golde and fee . . . .

Anon., *The playe of Robyn Hoode, verye proper to be played in Maye games,* first printed in the edition of *A mery geste of Robyn Hoode and of hys lyfe* of William Copeland in 1560. (See Sir W. W. Greg, *A bibliography of the English printed drama to the Restoration,* London, The Bibliographical Society, 1939, I, no. 32). See also Francis James Child, *The English and Scottish popular ballads,* III (1889), pp. 127-8 (illustrating his no. 123, 'Robin Hood and the Curtal friar', lines 85-110. My text is taken from The Tudor Facsimile Texts of 1914 (reprinted New York, 1970).

Note. Though some of the Robin Hood ballads refer to Kendal green as the clothing of Robin and his men, others refer to Lincoln green in this connection; see Child's nos. 117 – 'A gest of Robyn Hode', quatrain 422; 124 – 'The jolly Pinder of Wakefield', text B, stanza 4; 140 – 'Robin Hood rescuing three squires', text A, stanza 2; 149 – 'Robin Hood's birth, breeding, valor and marriage' (of Robin's mother), quatrain 10.

In Robin Hood's penultimate speech quoted above Child emended 'starte' to 'stare'. This reading is perhaps preferable.

4   [A Husbandman]   1577

Then was there yet another whom I see,
  Which stoode one of the hindmost of the route,
For soft, and no whit forthputting was hee;
  Full sunbrunt was his forehead and his snoute.

A man aboute a fiftie yeeres of age:
  Of kendall very course his coate was made.
My thought of truth his face was an image;
  upon his gyrdle hong a rustye blade.

. . . .

This was a husbandman, a simple hinde . . . .

Anonymous, *The debate betweene Pride and Lowlines, pleaded in an issue in Assise* . . . [London, 1577]. Edited by J. Payne Collier, London (Shakespeare Society), 1841, p. 33. Collier attributed the poem to Francis Thynne; according to a note in the new *Short-Title Catalogue* of English books printed before 1640 the attribution was mistaken – see vol. II, item 24061.

5   [A Serving Man's Clothes]   1581

Doctor. No doubte that is one great cause of the greater charge of householde. For I know when a Seruing man was co[n]tent to go in a Kendall coate in Sommer, and a frise cote in winter: and with a plaine white hose made meete for his body: And with a piece of biefe or some other dishe of sodde[n] meate all the weeke longe: Now he will looke to haue at the least for sommer a coate of the finest cloth that may bee gotten for money, and his Hosen of the finest Kersey, and of some straunge die, as Flaunders die or french puke, that a Prince or great Lord can weare no finer, if he weare cloth.

[Sir Thomas Smith], *A discourse of the common wealth of this realm of England* [1681]. I have used another edition of the same year, the title of which begins: *A compendious or briefe examination of certayn ordinary complaints, of diuers of our country men in these our dayes* . . . 1581, fo. 33v. Smith wrote the work in 1549; it was printed posthumously. There is a good modernised edition, based on both MSS and printed texts, by Mary Dewar, Charlottesville, 1969.

6   [Kendal]   1586

The Baronie of Kendale, id est, Baronia de Kendal, siue *Candalia,* id est, vallis ad Kanum nominatur, Kan enim fl. qui saxis asperatus hanc vallem perstringit, nomen indidit, ad cuius occiduam ripam frequentissimum oppidum Kandale, siue *Kirkeby Kandale,* id est fanum in valle ad Canum, duabus productis plateis se inter-secantibus sedet. Lanificij gloria & industria ita praecellens, vt eo nomine sit celeberrimum. Incolat enim copiosum, per vniuersam angliam, laneorum pannorum exercent mercaturam. Suoq; honori inprimis esse existimant, quod suos Barones, & Comites habuerint . . . .

William Camden, *Britannia,* London, 1586, pp. 447-8. For the English translation see no. 12 below.

7   [Falstaff's Misadventure]   ?1594

Fal[staf].   But as the diuell would haue it, three misbegotten knaues in Kendall greene came at my backe, and let driue at mee, for it was so darke Hal, that thou couldest not see thy hand.

Prin[ce].   These lies are like their father that begets them, grosse as a mountaine, open, palpable. Why thou clay braind guts, thou knotty-pated foole, thou horeson obscene greasie tallow-catch.

Falst.   What art thou mad? art thou mad? is not the truth the truth?

Pr.   Why how couldst thou know these men in Kendal greene when it was so darke thou couldst not see thy hand, come tell vs your reason. What sayst thou to this?

The historie of Henrie the Fourth: with the battel at Shrewsburie, between the King and Lord Henry Percy, surnamed Henrie Hotspur of the North. With the humorous conceits of Sir Iohn Falstaffe. London, 1598.

8   [The sturdy Ploughman]   1599

The sturdie Plough-man doth the soldier see,
All scarfed with pide colours to the knee,
Whom *Indian* pillage hath made fortunate,
And now he gins to loath his former state:
Now doth he inly scorne his Kendall-greene,
And his patch't Cockers now dispised beene.
Nor list he now go whistling to the Carre,
But sels his Teeme and fetleth to the warre.
O warre to them that neuer tryde thee sweete!
When his dead mate fals groueling at his feete,
And angry bullets whistlen at his eare,
And his dim eyes see nought but death and drere:
Oh happy Plough-man were thy weale well known;
Oh happy all estates except his owne!

I(oseph) H(all), *Virgidemiarum: The three last Bookes. Of byting Satyres.* London, 1599: lib. 4, sat. 6, lines 36-49, pp. 46-7.

9   [Robin Hood's Men and Prince John]   1600

[Scena ix]
Scar[let]. Its ful seauen years since we were outlawed first,
And wealthy Sherewood was our heritage:
For all those yeares we raigned vncontrolde:
From Barnsdale shrogs, to Notinghams red cliffes,
At Blithe and Tickhill were we welcome guests.
Good *George a Greene* at Bradford was our friend,
And wanton Wakefields Pinner lou'd vs well.
At Barnsley dwels a Potter tough and strong,
That neuer brookt, we brethren should haue wrong.
The Nunnes of Farnsfield, pretty Nunnes they bee,
Gaue napkins, shirts, and bands to him and mee.
Bateman of Kendall, gaue vs Kendall greene,
And *Sharpe* of Leeds, sharpe arrowes for vs made:
At Rotheram dwelt our bowyer, God him blisse,
Iackson he hight, his bowes did neuer misse.
This for our good, our scathe let *Scathlocke* tell,
In merry Mansfield, how it once befell.

16

[Scena xii]
[Prince Iohn] Southward I dare not flie: faine faine I would,
To Scotland bend my course: but all the woddes
Are full of Outlawes, that in Kendall greene,
Followe the outlawed earle of *Huntington,*
Well, I wil cloath my selfe in such a sute,
And by that meanes as well scape all pursuite,
As passe the daunger-threatning *Huntington*:
For hauing many outlawes theyl thinke mee,
By my attire, one of their mates to be.   Exit

. . . .

[Scena xv] Enter Prince *Iohn, solus,* in greene, bowe and arrowes.
Iohn. Why this is somewhat like, now may I sing,
As did the Wakefield Pinder in his note;
At Michaelmas commeth my couenant out,
    My master giues me my fee:
Then *Robin* Ile weare thy Kendall greene,
    And wend to the greenewodde with thee.

Anthony Munday, *The downfall of Robert Earl of Huntingdon* [i.e. Robin Hood], entered on
the Stationers' Register, 1 December, 1600 [printed 1601] edited by John C. Meagher, Oxford,
the Malone Society, 1964 (1965), lines 1279-95, 2071-80, 2507-12. The fragment sung by
Prince John at the end of the third extract is the earliest version known of the ballad of Robin
Hood and 'The jolly pinder of Wakefield', see Francis James Child, *The English and Scottish
Poplar Ballads,* III (1889), no. 124, pp. 129-32.

10   [Mourning for Robin Hood and Matilda]   1600

Fri[ar]. Here dothe the Frier leaue with grieuance:
Robin is dead, that grac't his entrance:
And being dead he craues his audience,
With this short play, they would haue patience.
                    Enter *Chester*.
Chest[er]. Nay Fryer, at request of thy kinde friend,
Let not thy Play so soone be at an end.
Though *Robin Hoode* be deade, his yeomen gone,
And that thou thinkst there now remaines not one.
To act an other Sceane or two for thee:
Yet knowe full well, to please this company,
We meane to end *Matildaes* Tragedie.
Fri[ar]. Off then, I wish you, with your *Kendall* greene:
Let not sad griefe, in fresh aray be seene.
Matildaes storie is repleat with teares,
Wrongs, desolations, ruins, deadly feares.
In, and attire yee: though I tired be,
Yet will I tell my mistresse Tragedie.

Anthony Munday, *The Death of Robert, Earle of Huntington. Otherwise called Robin Hood of merrie Sherwodde: with the lamentable Tragedie of chaste Matilda, his faire maid Marian, poysoned at Dunmowe by King John*. Entered on the Stationers' Register, 1 December, 1600, edited by John Meagher, Oxford, the Malone Society, 1965 (1967), lines 864-77.

11   [Kendal's Charter, her Trade and her Spiritual Needs]   1602

O that you would consider thankfully, that as our Gratious Soueraigne hath greatly graced you, in making your town of a country village, a corporate Borough, and vouchsafed to bestow vpon you a faire and large Charter for the establishing of your state of gouernment, and publike benefit of your populous multitude. So likewise that God himselfe hath as graciously blessed you in commending by his good prouidence your parish, for the spirituall cure and charge of your soules, to the patronage of so florishing a Colledge, & so fruitfull of learned preachers, that you may be certaine and sure, neuer to faile of a sufficient and vigilant pastour ouer you, and whereby noe doute you shall euermore co[n]tinew . . . . And would to God that as your towne is famous thorowgh the most partes of this Land, for your great trading lik a little Tirus, *for your meane yet n[ece]ssarie commodities for the common wealth: so your feruent zeale and fruitfull obedience vnto the word, were as faithfully showne heere & as famously*

18

knowne elsewhere, to your owne co[m]mendation and consolation of others, that with gratulation vnto God I might truly say of you and your people and the rest of my parish, as the Apostle Paul *of the Romans.* I. 8. I thanke my God thorough Iesus Christ for you all because your faith is published thorough the whole world . . . .

R.T. [=Ralph Tyrer, B.D., vicar of Kendal, 1592-1627], *Fiue godlie sermons . . .* London, 1602: Dedication to Iohn Smith, Alderman, and William Wilson, Senior Burgess, of Kendal and the rest of 'the Brethren, Gouernors, and Magistrates of the Burrough towne and corporation of Kendall'.

| 12 | [Kendal] | 1610 |

The Baronie of Kendale, that is, *The Dale by Can:* for it tooke name of the *riuer Can,* which running rough vpon stones cutteth through it: on the West banke whereof standeth *Kandale* or *Kendale,* called also *Kirkeby Kandale,* a towne of very great trade and resort, with two broad and long streets crossing the one over the other, and a place for excellent clothing and for industrie so surpassing, that in regard thereof it carrieth a great name: For, the inhabitants have great trafficke and vent of their wollen clothes throughout all parts of England. They count it also much for their credite, that it hath dignified Barons and Earles with the title thereof.

William Camden, *Britain,* London, 1610, p. 759, fo. 6R6r. Philemon Holland translated Camden's work into English.

| 13 | [The Mayor of Hartlepool] | 1611 |

. . . .

The Mayor of Hartlepoole vpon a day,
Hearing King *Harry* was to come that way,
Put on's considering cap, and Kendall gowne,
Consulting with his brethren of the Towne,
What gift they should present as he came by:
A Skatefish (quoth his Councell) sweet and dry:
Nay (quoth the Mayor) weele give him halfe one more:
Soft (quoth another) now your mouth runnes or'e:
"As there Masse Mayor, who could not doe but ore-doe,
"So *Coryate* here, he tels vs all, and more* too:

. . . .

[Marginal note of 1611:]   * Not more than truth, but more than other trauellers.

'Panegyrick verses' to Thomas Coryat's *Crudities Hastily gobled vp in fiue moneths trauells in France, Savoy, Italy, Rhetia commonly called the Grisons country, Helvetia alias Switzerland, some parts of high Germany and the Netherlands: Newly digested in the hungry aire of Odcombe in the County of Somerset, and now dispersed to the nourishment of the travelling Members of this Kingdome,* London, 1611, fo. e2^r.

In the dayes of King Henry the first, who was the first king that instituted the high court of Parliament, there liued nine men, which for the trade of Clothing, were famous throughout all England. Which Art in those dais was held in high reputation, both in respect of the great riches that therby was gotten, as also of the benefite it brought to the whole Common wealth: the yonger sons of knights and gentlemen, to whom their fathers would leaue no lands, were most commonly preferred to learne this trade, to the end that therby they might liue in good estate, & driue forth their daies in prosperity.

Among all Crafts, this was the only chiefe, for that it was the greatest marchandize, by the which our Countrey became famous through all Nations. And it was verily thought, that the one halfe of the people in the land liued in those daies therby, and in such good sort, that in the Common-wealth there was few or no beggars at all: poore people, whom God lightly blesseth with most children, did by meanes of this occupation so order them, that by the time that they were come to be sixe or seauen yeares of age, they were able to get their owne bread: Idlenesse was then banished our coast, so that it was a rare thing to heare of a thiefe in those dayes. Therefore it was not without cause that Clothiers were then both honoured and loued, among whom these nine persons in this Kings dayes were of great cedit, viz. [Thomas Cole of Reading, Gray of Gloucester, Sutton of Salisburie, Fitzallen of Worcester, Tome Doue of Exceter, and Simon of Southampton] alias *Supbroath*: who were by the King called, The sixe worthy husbands of the West. Then were there three liuing in the North, that is to say, *Cutbert* of Kendall, *Hodgekins* of Hallifax, and *Martin Byram* of Manchester. Euery one of these kept a great number of seruants at worke, spinners, carders, weauers, fullers, diars, sheeremen, and rowers, to the great admiration of all those that came into their houses to behold them.

[The six westerners came up to London in two groups of three after meeting at Basingstoke:] and the iij northerne Clothiers did the like, who commonly did not meet, till they came to Bosoms Inne in London.   [A2r-v]

....

[The day after the six arrived at the house of *Iarrat* the Gyant] they went to the hal, where they met the Northern clothiers, who greeted one another in this sort, What my maisters of the West, wel met: what cheere? what cheere? Euen the best cheere our Marchantes could make vs, (quoth *Gray*.). Then you could not chuse but fare well, quoth *Hogekins*: and you be weary of our company, adieu, quoth *Sutton*. Not so, sayd *Martin* but shall wee not haue a game ere see goe? Yes, faith for a hundred pounds. Well sayd, olde *Cole*, sayd they: and with that *Cole* and *Gray* went to the dice with *Martin* and *Hogekins*; and the dice running on *Hogekins* side, *Coles* money began to waste. Now by the Masse, quoth *Cole*, my mony shrinks as bad as northerne cloth. When they had played long, *Gray* stept to it and recouered the money that *Cole* had lost. But while they were thus playing, the rest being delighted in contrary matters, euery man satisfied his owne humor.

Tom Doue called for musicke, *VVilliam* of Worcester for wine, *Sutton* set his delight in hearing merry tales, *Simon* of South-hampton got him into the kitchen, and to the pottage pot he goes, for he esteemed more of a messe of pottage than of a venison pastie. Now sir, *Cutbert* of Kendall was of another minde, for no meate pleased him so wel as mutton, such as was laced in a red petticoate .... [Cutbert's affair with the wife of old Bosome of the eating-house then follows; it is entertaining, but it tells us nothing about the Kendal wool trade!]

(B1r-v)

....

And you shall vnderstand that when the country weauers, which came vp with their dames, saw the weauers of Candlewike-street, they had great desire presently to haue some conference with them, and thus one began to challenge thother for workmanship, quoth *VVeasell*, ile worke with any of you all for a crowne, take it if you dare, and he that makes his yeard of cloth soonest, shall haue it. You shall be wrought withall, said the other, and if it were for tenne crownes; but we wil make this bargaine, that each of vs shall wynde their owne quills. Content quoth *VVeasell*: and so to worke they went, but *VVesel* lost. Whereupon another of them tooke the matter in hand, who lost likewise: so that the London weauers triumphed against the country, casting forth diuers frumps.

Alas poore fellowes, quoth they, your hearts are good, but your hands are ill. Tush, the fault was in their legges, quoth another, pray you friend were you not borne at home? Whie doe you aske quoth *VVeasell*? because, said hee, the biggest place of your legge is next to your shoe.

Cutbert hearing this, being cholericke of nature, chafed like a man of law at the barre, and he wagers with them foure crowns to twain, the others agreed, to work they go: but *crab* conquered them all.

Whereupon, the London weauers were nipt in the head like birds, and not a word to say.

Now saith *Crab* as we haue lost nothing, so haue won nothing, and because I know ye cannot be right weauers, except you be good fellowes, therefore if you will go with vs, wee will bestow the ale vpon you. That is spoken like a good fellow and like a weauer, quoth the other. So along they went as it were to the signe of the red Crosse.

(D3v-4r)

....

Hodgekins of Halifax did also great good, so did *Cutbert* of Kendall, who had married xxiij. couples out of his owne house, giuing each of them X. li. to beginne the world withall. *Martin Byram* of Manchester gaue toward the building of a free schoole in Manchester, a great masse of money. And thus (gentle Reader) haue I finished my Stories of these worthy men, desiring thee to take my paines in good part, which will incourage me to greater matters, perceiuing this curteously accepted. (K2v)

FINIS.

T[homas] D[eloney], *Thomas of Reading. Or, The sixe worthy yeomen of the West.* Now the fourth time corrected and enlarged by T. D. Printed at London for T.P. 1612. I have used the facsimile edition of the Scolar Press, Menston, England, 1969, checked against the original in the British Library. Earlier editions than the fourth have not survived. The name of Cuthbert of Kendal recurs in our no. 18. For the gibes by Cole about the shrinking of Northern cloth, see our no. 15 and the appendix.

15   [Kendal Cottons and their Problems]   1615

To all true-bred Northerne Sparks, of
the generous society of the Cottoneers, who
hold their High-roade by the Pinder of *Wake-*
field, the Shoo-maker of *Brandford* [sic], and
the white Coate of Kendall: Light gaines,
Heauie Purses, good Tradings,
with cleere Conscience.   p. 189

43 Then, my deere countrimen, to giue your due,
From whence comes mans perfection, but from you.   p. 190
That doe maintaine with credit your estate,
And sells the best of man at easie rate,
To wit, the minds resemblance, which is gotten,
By those same *linings which you sell of Cotten.*
For see those thin breech Irish lackies runne,
50 How small i'th wast, how sparing in the bombe,
VVhat *Iacke a Lents* they are: yet view them when
They haue beene lin'd by you, theyr proper men,
Yea I may say, man is so strange an Elfe,
54 VVithout your helpe, hee lookes not like himselfe.   p. 191

89 Next I expresse your worth in, shall be these,
90 *First, your supportance of poore families,*
Which are so weake in state, as I much doubt me,
They would be forc't to begge or starue without ye.
The second is, (wherein you'ue well deserued,
The care you haue to see your Countrey serued,
Not as such men who liue by forraine Nations,
Impouerishing this Land by transportations,
For their depraued Nature be well showne,
By louing strangers better then their owne;
Or as it seemes, to sucke their Mothers bloud,
100 Their Natiue Countrie for a priuate good.
The third and last, which heere exprest shall be,
Shall reference haue to your *Antiquity,*
All which I will dilate of, and though I
Cannot describe ech thing so mouingly,   p. 192
As I could wish, yet take it in good part,
Proceeding from the centre of my heart,

23

That did this taske and labour vndertake,
For your *profession* and your *countries* sake,
Whose ayre I breath'd, O I were worthy death,
110 *Not to loue them, who suck't with me one breath.*
How many *Families* supported be,
Within the compasse of one *Barronry,*
By your profession I may boldly show,
(For what I speake, I by obseruance know.)
Yea by eye-witnesse, where so many are,
Prouided for by your peculiar care,
As many would the beggars be (I wot)
If your religious care releeu'd them not.
For there young brats, as we may well suppose,
120 Who hardly haue the wit to don their clothes,
Are set to worke, and well can finish it,
Being such labours as doe them befit:
Winding of spooles, or such like easie paine,
By which the least may pretty well maintaine
Themselues, in that same simple manner clad,
As well agrees with place where they were bred.
Each plies his worke, one cards, another spins,
One to the studdles goes, the next begins
To rauell for new wefte, thus none delay,
130 *But make their webbe-vp, 'gainst each Market-day,*
For to preserue their credit: but pray see,
Which of all these for all their industry,
Their early rising, or late sitting vp,
Could get one bit to eat, or drop [?to] suppe.   p. 193
If hauing wrought their *webbes,* their forc't to stand,
And not haue you to take them off their hand.
And now by th'way, that I my loue may shew,
Vnto the *poorer sort* as well as you,
Let me exhort you, in respect I am,
140 Vnto you all both *friend and Countriman,*
And one that wisheth, if hee could expresse,
What's wishes be vnto your *Trade* successe,
As to himselfe, these *poore men* (vnder fauour)
Who earne their meanes so truly by their labour,
Should not (obserue me) bee enforc't to wait
"For what you owe, and what's their due, so late,
Time vnto them is pretious, *yea one houre,*

24

If idlye spent, is charges to the poore:
Whose labour's their Reuenue: doe but goe,
150 To *Salomon,* and he will tel you so . . . .

                                                              p. 194

169 But in transferring of the charge to such,
170 As be your *Factors,* which haue had small tutch
     Of others griefes: your selues haue had the blame,
     Though't seems your *Factors* well deseru'd the same.
     Nor would I haue you thinke Ime fed for this,
     For they do plead in *Forma pauperis*
     That bee my *Clyents,* yea Ime tied too,
     In countries loue to doe that which I doe:
     For euen their teares, mones, and distressed state,
     Haue made me for them so compassionate,
     That my soule yearn'd within me, but to heare,
180 Their mones despisd, that were esteem'd so deere,
     To their *Creator,* see their Image then;
     And make recourse to him that gaue it them,
     Whose mansion is aboue the highest sphere,
     And bottles vp the smallest trickling teare,
     Shed by the poorest soule, (which in a word)
     Shall in that glorious synod beare record:
     Where for the least non-payment which we owe,
188 Shall passe this doome – *Away ye cursed, goe.*   p. 195

203 VVell it appeares, euen by your proper worth,
     That you were borne for her that brought you forth,
     Not for yourselues, which instanced may be,
     In that you ayme at no *Monopoly,*
     No *priuate staples,* but desire to sell,
     (VVhich of all other seem's approu'd as well,)
     Your *Ware* in publique places, which may stand
210 No more for your auaile, then good of th'land.
     Nor are you carelesse what it is you bring,
     Vnto your *Countrey,* for your customing,
     Dependance has vpon that due esteeme,
     They haue of you, that are the same you seem,
     Plaine home-bred chapmen (yet of such due note)
     Their word is good, how plaine so ere's their coat.
     Yea doe I wish I may haue such as they,
     Ingag'd to me, for they'l do what they say,

When silken coats, and some of them I know,
220 *Will say farre more then ere they meane to doe.*
    Therefore it much concernes you to produce,
    That which you know is for a common vse.
    Not for the eye so much as for the proofe,
    For this doth tend most to your owne behoofe: p. 196
    VVhere Reputation doth such custome gaine,
    As being got is seldome lost againe.
    Yet sure methinks *my Friends,* you put to th'venture,
    VVhen your commodities are stretcht on th'tenter,
    So that as I haue heard, when come to weting
230 *They shrinke a yard at least, more then is fitting.*
    Yet doe I heare you make excuse of this.
    That for your selues you know not what it is:
    And for your *Factors* what they take, they pay,
    If *Shere-men* stretch them so, the more knaues they.
    It's true they are so, yet for all you vse
    These words, beleeu't, they'l serue for no excuse,
    For if you will be common-weales men, know,
    VVether your *Shere-men* vse this feate or no,
    Before you buy, (which found) reprooue them then,
240   Or else auoid such tenter-hooking men.
    There is a Gallant in this towne I know
    (Who damnd himselfe, but most of them doe soe)
    If that he had not, to make cloake and suit,
    Some thirty yards of rug or thereabout,
    Yet hardly came to fifteene afterward,
    It had beene measur'd by the Taylors yard.
    Now was not this too monstrous and to badde,
    That it should leese ffull halfe of that it had?
    I know not what to thinke (but to be breefe)
250   Either the Taylor was an arrant theefe,
    And made no bones of Theft, which is a crime,
    Most Taylors will dispence with at this time:
    Or sure, if my weake wit can iudge of it,
254   The rugge was *tentred* more then did befit: . . .   p. 197

277   "Now to the *third Branch,* is my muse addrest,
278   To make your *Trades* Antiquity exprest . . .   p. 198

[The classical weaver *Carmentis* came to England, arriving at

Workington, made her way via Cartmel (or *Carment-hill*) to the
valley of the Kent]

357 *Downe from the neighbouring Mountaines, she might spie,*
A woody vale, seat'd deliciously,
Through which a pleasant Riuer seemd to glide,

366 *VVhich did this vale in equall parts deuide,*
This hauing spide, (on Stauelaies Cliffes *they say)*
She laid her staffe, whence comes the name Staffe-lay.
Corruptly Staulay, *where she staid a space,*
But seeing it a most notorious place,
And that the trades men were so giuen to th' Pot,
That they would drinke far more then ere they got.
She turnd from thence, yet left some Maids behinde,
That might acquaint them in this wool worke kinde.
VVhile she did plant, as ancient Records be,

370 *Neerer to* Kendall *in th' Barronrie.*

. . . .

374 . . . the erection of your *Sturbidge* [sic] *faire.*   p. 201
I thought to shadow briefely, which began,
On this occasion by a *Kendall* man,
Who comming vp or downe I know not well,
Brought his commodities that way to sell:
Where being benighted, tooke no other shield,

380 *To lodge him and his ware then th' open field:*
A Mastiffe had he, or a mungril Cur,
Which he still cride and cald on, Stur-bitch stur,
Least miching knaues now fore the spring of day,
Should come perchance, and filch his ware away.

385 From hence they say tooke *Sturbidge* first her name . . .   p. 292

. . . .

467 *"Descending thither where most bound I am,*
"To Kendall-white-coates, *where your trade began.*
Kendall (to which I all successe do wish)

470 May termed be that parts *Metropolis,*
For seate as pleasant, as the most that are,
Instanc't in th' ruin'd *Castle of Lord Par,*
(For seate imparaled); where we may see,

474 "Great men to fall as subject are as we . . . .   p. 205

. . . .

[A eulogy of Kendal follows, her wealth in a small compass, her
pure air, her climate, the river Kent, with clear water that boils

27

quickly, her woods formerly plentiful but now cut down through the egotism of man, praise of her parson, Ralph Tyrer, B.D.]

529 Now must I haue the *White-coates* vnder-hand
530 Who were in fore-time a defence to th' land:
Yea such they were, as when they did appeare,
They made their foes *perfume their hose for feare,*
Experiens't *Archers,* and so practis'd it,
As they would seldome shoot but they would hit.   p. 206
So that th' darters of rude *Scythia,*
The *golden-Archers* of rich *Persia,*
The *Siluer-shields* of *Greece* haue borne the name,
Blaz'd by the partiall trumpe of lying fame.
Yet in behalfe of *Kendall* (I durst sweare it)
540 For true renovvne these *Countries* came not nere it,
As for this name of *white-coate* vs'd to fore
It came from th' *milk-white furniture they wore*
And in good-sooth they vvere but home-spun fellovvs
"Yet would these *white-coats* make their foes dy yellows,
VVhich might by latter times be instanced,
546 Euen in those border-seruices they did . . . .   p. 207

. . . .

[He then returns to the faults of the men of Kendal mentioned above and warns them of god's judgment on evil-doers, urges them to give money to the poor, to pay proper wages and not to abuse the tenters. When they have been so good they can afford to be happy; he pictures their songs and dances and mentions 'VVilsons delight', 'Arthura Bradley' and 'Mal Dixons round'. Then he praises the virtue, intelligence and social gifts of a Kendal man, whom he leaves unnamed. At length this long poem ends with a final couplet:]

611 But th'Euening shade drawes on, and damps the light
612 "Think friends on what I sayd, and so good night.   p. 210

From Richard Brathwait, *A Strappado for the Diuell,* (London, 1615) ed. J. W. Ebbsworth, Boston, Lincolnshire, 1878, pp. 189-210.

16   [Kendal]   1622

Where *Westmerland* to West, by wide *Wynander* Mere,
The *Eboracean* fields her to the Rising bound,
Where Can first creeping forth, her feet hath scarcely found,
But giues that Dale her name, where *Kendale* towne doth stand,
For making of our Cloth scarce match'd in all the land.

Michael Drayton, *Poly-olbion*, London, 1622. *The thirtieth Song*, fo. Y1r, p. 161.

17   [Kendal Wool Work and the Family]   1615

Againe, in our *Townes* lying further within Land, the inhabitants use some especiall Trade to keepe their *Youth* in labour; whereby they become not only beneficiall to themselves, but usefull and helpfull unto others. Amongst which, I cannot be unmindfull of the diligence of the Towne of *Kendall,* and worthy care which they have to see their very young children put to work, being a labour which requires no great strength, to wit, *Wooll-worke.* Wherein, so approved hath their care and industrie beene, as they have gained no small esteeme in forraine places, who are made partakers of the fruit of their labours. For I have known a familie, consisting of seven or eight persons, maintained by the work of two or three stones of wooll, which amounted not above thirty shillings: and with this they maintained credit, living in an honest and decent manner. Whose labours as they were laudable, so have they been no lesse furthered, favoured, and encouraged by our late gracious Soveraigne of renow[n]ed memory; who, of his princely clemencie, hath dammed all such impositions or heavy taxations as might any way impaire or impeach the free use of that Trade. Albeit now of late, the Towne of *Kendall,* so famous for *Wooll-worke,* by reason of a late decrease or decay of Trade in those parts, is growne no lesse penurious than populous: so as (with griefe I speake it) such inhabitants as formerly by their paine and industrie were able to give an almes at their doore, are now forced to begge their almes from doore to doore. The redresse whereof, as it hath beene by the Prince and those prudent guides and guardians of our State, the Lords of his Privie Counsell, duley intended; so no doubt, but by their wise care it shall be accordingly effected, & those poore people after so many miseries sustained, wholly releeved; for the advancement of Gods glory, the supportance of many a needfull family, and the succeeding renowne of his Majesty, to whom every subject oweth his life, love and loyalty.

Richard Brathwait, *The English Gentleman . . .* London, 1630, pp. 125-6 (fos. R3r-v).

Amongst all the crue of *George* [*a Green* – the Pinder of Wakefield] his mad companions, he selected halfe a dozen of lusty fellowes for to accompany him in all his pastimes and merriments, which were as officers vnder him . . . hauing whetted their wits with a little nappy ale, *George a Greene* began to make this oration following to his Souldiers, Louing friends and Countreymen, . . . seeing it hath pleased you out of your loues and good wills that you beare me, to chuse me for your Captaine and commander you shall finde me euer ready at all times to the vtmost of my power in all honest attempts ready and diligent, now on the other side I must request you also according to your places you are now chosen in to be carefull therein, and chiefly to obserue these following orders . . . . Thirdly, any man foote or horse that went through the towne of *Wakefield* with a long staffe on his necke, to make them trayle it after them, or else to haue a bout at Sword and Buckler, or else to lay down there twelue pence . . . .   [pp. 5-6]

Of a great fray that hapned in *Wakefield*
betwixt *Kendall* men, *Hallifax* men and *George*
and his companions.

There dwelt in the *North* two welthy Yeomen, which dealt much in cloathing, namely, *Cuthbert* of *Kendall* and *Hoskins* of *Hallifax*, which kept lusty waine-men to goe with their cloth from place to place. It was their chance to come through *Wakefield* with their long staues on their necks, which *Tobit* the thresher perceiuing called vnto them, saying, Down with your staues, for you must beare them so vp: and so stepping to them shewed them their orders, saying, if that you cannot reade I will reade them vnto you, and if you cannot vnderstand them I will make you vnderstand them: what a prating keepes the knaue, quoth the men? art thou out of thy wits? Out of my wits, quoth he, you are deceiued, and that you shall finde presently, with that he steps hardly, and fetcht out the Quarter staues, and long staues with the other of the weapons. Down with your staues I say, or else you must haue a bout or two with me at these weapons. Stay the carts, quoth a *Kendall* man, I warrant you that he shall haue his belly full. And so to it they went stiffely; but *Tobit* layd about him so stoutly that he made the *Kendall* man giue ouer and lay downe his weapons. Come another, quoth *Tobit*, stay not: another came and to their busines close they went, but *Tobit* behaued himselfe so well that hee broke the pate of him, which the *Kendall* and *Hallifax* men perceiuing their fellowes to be beaten, all of them at once came vpon *Tobit*; but he defended himselfe stoutly against them all. In the meane time came *Miles* the Miller, *Tom* the Taberer, *Smug* the Smith with the rest of the crue, and seeing all vpon *Tobit*, this is foule play and amongst them they all rushed, insomuch that such a fray was hardly seene in *Wakefield* many yeeres before: the Townsmen they rung the Common bell, which *George a Greene* perceiuing, he came running to know the newes, and knowing it came amongst the hottest of them laying about him manfully, vntill at last he had made the poore *Kendall* men and *Hallifax* men lay downe their staues, and yet they were in all a dozen of proper fellowes. Nay you haue not done yet, quoth *George,* looke vpon the orders, down with your staues, and dril and draw them after you through the Towne: the which poore men they willingly did, and so they departed with heauy hearts and broken pates and shinnes, vowing to be reuenged, withall threatning them to come againe: and withall challeng'd *George* and his companions to play with them on Midsummer day next coming at all manner of weapons whatsoeuer, especially those that follow, . . . [Next day they had a football match in the morning, wrestling in the afternoon and both sides drank together, 'they did liquor there insides as well as they had their outsides basted, and so they departed, each taking leaue of one another in kindly manner with a faithfull promise on each side not to faile on Midsummer day.']   [pp. 8-9]

[The account of the Midsummer contests is given in the beginning of *The Second Part* –
pp. 53-6.]

The Pinder of Wakefield: Being the merry History of George a Greene the lusty Pinder of the North.
Briefly shewing his manhood and his braue merriments amongst his boone companions. A Pill fit to purge
melancholy in this drooping age. With the great battel fought betwixt him and Robin Hood, Scarlet and
Little Iohn, and after of his liuing with them in the Woods. Full of pretty Histories, Songs, Catches, Iests,
and Ridles. [London, 1632.] Edited by E. A. Horsman, Liverpool, 1956.

19   [Lament for the Kendal shearmen drowned in   1636
      Windermere on 19 October, 1635]

THE FATALL NVPTIALL:
OR,
MOVRNFVLL
MARRIAGE.

....

Windermere, *or* Winandermere, . . . *hath ever constantly kept a Boat for Passengers; especially those Inhabitants as remaine or reside in the Barronry of* Kendall, *(a place to her honour, antiently famous for Commerce and industrious Manufacture) as all others, who may have occasion to address their course by that passage, to the Market of* Haukeside [i.e. Hawkshead], *or other places adjoyning. To this Boat, upon a* nuptiall *but* fatall *occasion, sundry Passengers, and these all inhabitants within the Barronry of* Kendall, *(a Burrough as I formerly observed, highly eminent, by having such neare relation and generall correspondence with most places of trade or trafficke in this kingdome) repaired, hoping with a safe and secure gale to arrive, where no perill had ever yet approach'd . . . .*

....

  But let me now divert my dolefull Scene,
  And pencyle these who now have drowned bene:
  In their owne native feature! "These were such
  Who to relieve their Meniey, labour'd much
  In their industrious wool-worke, justly fam'd,
  And for their Manuall labour *Sheare-men* nam'd.
  An usefull mystery! which though it make
  Course cloaths, and such as ne're did *Alnage* take,
  Yet 'tis commodious to the Common-weale,
  And fit for Sale, although unfit for Seale,
  For if th'poore work-man scarcely can supply
  With late and early toile his Family
  Now when his trading is exempt and freed,
  In paying *Alnage* how should hee succeede?
  But Heav'ns be blest for our dread Soveraigne,
  Who cheeres with freedom such an honest gaine.

....

[Richard Brathwait], *The Fatall Nuptiall*, London, 1636, fos. A2v-3r; A8v-B1r. (See W. G. Collingwood, '*The Fatall Nuptiall* a tract (by Richard Brathwaite?) on the Windermere Ferry Accident of 1635', CW2 XIII (1913), 147-59.

20   [Kendal]   1638

Nunc ad Kendall, *propter *pannum,*
Coetum, situm †Aldermannum,
Virgines pulchras, pias matres,
Et viginti quatuor fratres,
Verè clarum & beatum,
Mihi nactum, notum, natum.

Now to *Kendall,* for *Cloth-making,
Sight, site †*Alderman* awaking;
Beauteous Damsels, modest mothers,
And her foure and twenty brothers,
Ever in her honour spreading,
Where I had my native breeding.

* *Lanificii gloria, & industria [ita]*
praecellens, ut eo nomine sit celeberrimum.
Cam[den] *in* Brit[ania].
Pannus mihi panis. *Mot[to].*

* A Towne so highly renouned for her
commodious cloathing, and industrious
Trading, as her name is become famous
in that kind. *Cam[den]* in *Brit[ain]*.
Cloth is my bread. Mot[to].

† *Nomine* Major *eas, nec sis minor omine*
sedis, Competat ut titulo civica vita novo.

† Now hast thou chang'd they title into
May're, Let life, state, style improve thy
charter there.

Barnabees Journall. Under the names of Mirtilus & Faustulus shadowed: for the Travellers solace lately
published, to most apt numbers reduced, and to the old tune Barnabe commonly chanted. By Corymboeus.
[Undated, no imprint. Unpaged. By Richard Brathwait, London, 1638] Fo. CC7v & Cc8r.

21   [Stourbridge Fair]   1655

IV. 36. This *Sturbridge-fair* is so called from *Stur,* a little *Rivolet* (on
both sides whereof it is kept) on the *East* of *Cambridge,* whereof this
Original is reported. A *Clothier* of *Kendale,* a Town* charactered to be
Lanificii gloria, & industria praecellens, casually wetting his *Cloath* in that
water in his passage to *London,* exposed it there to sail, on cheap termes,
as the worse for the wetting; and yet it seems saved by the bargain.
Next year he returned again, with some other of his townsmen,
profering *drier* and *dearer* Cloath to be sold; so that within a few yeares,
hither came a confluence of *Buyers, Sellers,* and *Lookers on,* which are the
three *Principles* of a Fair. In *Memoriall* whereof, *Kendale-men* challenge
some priviledge in that place, annually chusing one of the town to be
Chief, before whom an antick *Sword* was carried with some mirthfull
Solemnities; disused of late, since these *sad times,* which put mens minds
into more *serious Imployments.*

37. It is at this day the most plentifull of Wares in all *England,* (most
fairs in other places being but Markets in comparison thereof;) being an
Amphibion, as well *going* on *Ground,* as *swimming* by *Water,* by the
benefit of a *navigable River.*

Thomas Fuller, *A History of the University of Cambridge,* London, 1655, p. 66, fo. 51lv.
* Camd. Brit. in Westmorland.

22   [Aeneas in Kendal Breeches]   1665

No sprightly Groom so trim and trick is,
That just upon preferments prick is,
As was *Æneas*, stories say,
When clad in cloaths of Holy-day.
    His breeches sav'd from *Troys* combustion
Were Kendal, and his Doublet Fustian:
Pinck't with most admirable grace,
And richly laid with green-silk lace . . . .

Charles Cotton, *Scarronides: or Virgile Travestie. A Mock-Poem. In imitation of the Fourth Book of Virgils Æneis in English, Burlesque*. London, 1665, pp. 30-1 (fols. B8ᵛ-C1ʳ).

23   [The Needs of Kendal Tradesmen]   1665

THE Shire-Town is *Apleby*, which merits preeminence onely for antiquity: for *Kendall*, being the Garrison-Town for the County, has been ever renowned for her affluence of commerce, and confluence of People: Being a *Burgess* highly fam'd for her *Manufactory* in *Woolwork*: which, by their experienc'd industry, became infinitely commodious to the *Corporation* and Parts adjacent: though of late much decreasing. Which it were to be wish'd, that it might be timely supplied, and cheerfully reviv'd, by the assistance and application of those Members in the High Court of Parliament, who stand obliged, upon their Election, to promote the *Interests* of their Countrey; by removing all probable occurencies, that may obstruct the improvement of it. An imployment, no doubt more corresponsive to their Place, whereto they are, by the Votes and Voices of their Countrey, deputed; than any *Self-seeking-Interest*, wherewith, I hope, that sharp *Northern ayr* will not suffer them to be infected.

Richard Brathwait, *The interest of Westmerland* in *The Captive-Captain*, London, 1665, pp. 177-8.

34

Kendall, or rather Kirkby Kendale (writ antiently Kirkby in Kendale, i.e. the church town in Kendale[)]. It is the chief town for largeness, neatness, buildings and trade in this county, and is most pleasantly seated, for the most part on the west bank of the river Kent, so called from Kent-meer in this county, where its head is, which river gave name to a fruitful vale called Kent-Dale, wherein this town is placed, and to Kent-Sands in Lancashire, this town gave name to the whole Barony . . . . This town is seated in very good air, and its healthfulness is improved partly by the cleanliness of the people, and partly by its situation on a hill side, the river carrying away whatever filthiness the descending rain washeth out of it. It hath two broad and long streets, fairly built, crossing the one over the other, 2 large stone bridges, and one of wood. It hath also a fair church . . . . [p. 6]

This town is a place of excellent manufacture, and for civility, ingenuity, and industry so surpassing, that in regard thereof it deservedly carrieth a great name. The trade of the town makes it populous, and the people seem to be shaped out for trade, improving themselves not only in their old manufactures of cottons, but of late of making of drugget, serges, hatts, worsted, stockings, &c., whereby many of the poor are daily set on work, and the town much enriched. The inhabitants are generally addicted to sobriety and temperance, and express a thriftiness in their apparel, the women using a plain tho' decent and handsome dress, above most of their neighbours . . . .

Sir Daniel Fleming of Rydal, *A description of Westmoreland* . . . Compiled Anno Christi, M.DC.LXXI. Edited by Sir G. F. Duckett, Bart. London & Kendal, 1882, p. 8.

25   [Kendal]   1692

On the western bank of the River Kent stands Kendal, as it is commonly called, it is anciently written Kirkby in Kendal, which consists of two streets of considerable length intersecting each other. It is a most famous town for its industry and the woollen trade, for its inhabitants sell their cottons to most parts of England . . . . Their trade consists of Kendal cogware, alias cottons, of Lindsey wools or Kendal stuffs which // are otherwise called Kidderminsters, from being sold there, and of stockings . . . (which at this time keeps a great many children at work). And all these wares are sent to London every week by four Kendal carriers who set out from thence every Monday by turns.

Thomas Machell, *Collections towards a history of the Barony of Kendal* in Jane M. Ewbank, *Antiquary on Horseback,* C&WA&AS, Extra series, XIX, pp. 60-1.

26   [Kendal cottons]   1702

Kendall is a town built all of stone, one very broad streete in which is the Market Crosse, its a goode tradeing town mostly famed for the cottons; Kendall Cotton is used for blanckets and the Scotts use them for their plodds and there is much made here and also linsiwoolseys and a great deale of leather tann'd here and all sorts of commodityes twice a weeke is the market furnished with all sorts of things.

Celia Fiennes, *The Journeys,* edited by Christopher Morris, London, The Cresset Press, 1947, p. 191 (from 'My Great Journey to Newcastle and to Cornwall', 1698).

APPENDIX

Other texts about the frauds in woollen manufacture

i

And that which is here spoken of wine, he meaneth it of al actes in the cytye, of al kindes of faculties, for they haue al theyr medles and mynglynges. That he speaketh of one thynge, he meaneth generally of al. I must tell you more newes yet.

I here saye, there is a certayne connyng come vp in myxyng of wares.

Howe saye you, were it not wonder to here that clothe makers should become poticaries[?].

Yea and as I heare saye, in suche a place, where as they haue professed the Gospell, and the word of God most earnextly of a longe tyme. Se how busie the Deueil is to sclaunder the word of god? Thus the pore gospel goeth to wracke. Yf his clothe by xviii. yerdes longe, he wyl set hym on a racke, and streach hym out with ropes, and racke hym tyll the senewes shrinke a gayne, whyles he hath brought hym to xxvii. yardes. When they haue brought him to that perfection, they haue a pretty feate to thycke him againe. He makes me apouder for it, an[d] playes the poticary, thei cal it floke pouder they do so in corporate it to the cloth, that it is wonderfull to consider, truely a goodly inuention.

Oh that so goodly wittes shold be so yl applyed, they maye wel deceyue the people but they can not deceyue God. They were wont to make beddes of flockes and it was a good bed to, nowe they haue turned theyr flockes into a pouder to playe the false theaues with it. O wicked deuil what can he inuent to blaspheme Goddes worde? These myxtures come of couetousnes. Thei are playne theft. Woo worthe that these flockes should so slander the worde of God.

As he saied to the Iewes, thy wyne is myngled wyth water, so myghte he haue sayed to vs of thys Lande. Thy clothe is myngeled wyth flockepouder.

Hugh Latimer, *The thyrde Sermon . . . whyche he preached before the Kynge within hys graces Palayce at Westmister* [sic] *the .xxii. daye of Marche.* In *Seven Sermons before Edward VI. On each Friday in Lent, 1549.* Edited by Edward Arber, Westminster, 1895, pp. 86-7.

37

ii

Theodorus. I thinke there is great fault to bee found in the first makers of the cloth, for the naughtinesse thereof, as well as in the Drapers, is there not?

Amphilogus. No doubt of that. For some put in naughty wool, and cause it to be spun & drawne into a very small thred, and then compounding with the Fuller to thicke it very much, and with the Clothier also to sheare it very lowe, and with some liquide matter to lay downe the wooll so close, as you can hardly see any wale, and then selleth it as though it were a very fine cloth indeed. Other some mixe good wooll and naughty wooll togither, and vsing it as before, they will sell it for principall good cloth, when it is no thing lesse. And then for their further aduantage, euery vaine, euery ioint, and euery thred must be so tentered and racked, as I warrant it for euer being good after. Now, it being thus tentered at his hands, and after at the Drapers handes, I pray you how should this cloth be ought or endure long?

Phillip Stubbes, *The Second part of the Anatomie of Abuses, containing The display of Corruptions* . . . London, 1583. (Edited by Frederick J. Furnivall, London, 1877-9, second pagination, p. 24. Furnivall quotes législation of the reigns of Elizabeth I and of James I against such practices – pp. xiv† – xv†.)

iii

Honisuckle. They saye Charing-Crosse is falne downe, since I wente to *Rochell*: but thats no such wonder, twas old, and stood awry (as most part of the world can tell.) . . . Charing-corsse was olde, and olde thinges must shrinke as well as new Northern cloth.

Thomas Decker and John Webster, *Westward Hoe*, II. i, pp. 35-42. (I quote from *The Dramatic Works of Thomas Dekker*, edited by Fredson Bowers, II, Cambridge, 1955, p. 331.)

Lodouico. Gentlemen, you all know *Signior Candido*, the Linnen Draper, he that's more patient then a browne baker, vpon the day when he heates his Ouen, and forty Scolds about him.

Omnes. Yes, we know him all, what of him?

Lodouico. Wud it not be a good fit of mirth, to make a piece of English cloth of him, and to stretch him on the Tainters, till the threds of his owne naturall humor cracke, by making him drinke healths, Tobacco, dance, sing bawdy songs, or to run any bias according as we thinke good to cast him?

Carolo. 'Twere a Morris dance worth the seeing.

Thomas Dekker, *The honest whore, part 2*, IV. iii, pp. 15-24. (*Ed. cit.*, p. 197.)

GLOSSARY

(After each definition I give the number of the item in which the words occur and the name of the author where he can be identified.)

Alnage = the duty on measuring cloth by the ell or yard by a sworn officer who inspected and sealed woollen cloth. 19 (Brathwait 3).

Barronry = Barony, the Barony of Kendal. 6, 12 (Camden 1 and 2), 15 (Brathwait 1, lines 112, 370), 19 (Brathwait 3), 24 (Fleming).

be lykelyhood = probably. 2 (Leland).

bombe = bum, 'the part on which we sit' (Dr. Johnson's definition). 15 (Brathwait 1, line 50).

Burgess = a burgess town, i.e. one with full municipal rights. 23 (Brathwait 5).

Can (or *Kan*) = the river Kent. 6, 12 (Camden 1 and 2), 16 (Drayton).

Candale (or *Candalia* or *Kandalia*) = Kendal. 6, 12 (Camden 1 and 2).

carders = those who card (see the next item below) wool. 14 (Deloney).

cards = uses the instrument with which the wool was combed to raise the nap on the cloth or in preparing the wool. 15 (Brathwait 1, line 126).

cockers = leggings or a combination of high boots and gaiters. 8 (Hall).

Cotten (or *cottons*) = the coarse woollen cloth made in Kendal and other northern parts. Bouch and Jones tell us that the name was derived from the process of 'cottoning' or raising the nap on the cloth (p. 140n). It is not derived from 'coatings', a word not current until 1770. 15 (Brathwait 1, line 48), 24 (Fleming), 25 (Machell), 26 (Fiennes).

Cottoneers = those who dealt in cottons. 15 (Brathwait 1, title).

Cut and bause = ? 3 (anonymous).

drere = drear (noun), i.e. dread, terror. 8 (Hall).

drugget = coarse woollen stuff used for floor or table covering. 24 (Fleming).

Eboracean = of Yorkshire. 16 (Drayton).

fetleth = fettles himself, gets himself ready or prepares himself. 8 (Hall).

forthputting = putting himself forward. 4 (anonymous).

frise = frieze, a coarse woollen cloth, with the nap only on one side. 5 (Smith).

frumps = insults. 14 (Deloney).

fullers = those who clean and thicken cloth. 14 (Deloney).

hinde = a peasant, a countryman. 4 (anonymous).

hose (or *hosen*) = breeches. 5 (Smith), 15 (Brathwait 1, line 533).

Iacke-a-Lents = male Aunt Sallies, thin inconspicuous people. 15 (Brathwait 1, line 51).

Kan, see *Can* above.

kersey = a coarse narrow cloth made of short wool, usually ribbed. 5 (Smith).

Lanificij gloria, & industria ita praecellens . . . = the glory of wool men and an industry so surpassing . . . 6 (Camden 1), 20 (Brathwait 4), 21 (Fuller).

linsiwoolseys = linseywoolsey, cloth made originally of linen and wool mixed. 26 (Fiennes).

longging = belonging. 2 (Leland).

Masse = Master. 13 (Richmond).

Meniey = meinie, household, family. 19 (Brathwait 3).

miching = stealing, pilfering. 15 (Brathwait 1, line 383).

Moles = masses, obstacles. 2 (Leland).

nappy = frothy, heady, strong. 18 (anonymous).

paine = labour, toil, pains. 17 (Brathwait 2).

Paroch = parish. 2 (Leland).

Pinck't = pinked, pierced with small holes, adorned. 22 (Cotton).

plucke = ?a pull, a draw – here, probably, a fight. 3 (anonymous).

plodds = plaids. 26 (Fiennes).

puke = a superior kind of cloth from which gowns were made; colour of cloth produced by galls or copperas. 5 (Smith).

quilles = quills, the reed on which weavers wind their threads, a bobbin. 14 (Deloney).

rauell = ravel, to disentangle. 15 (Brathwait 1, line 129).

rowers = ? 14 (Deloney).

rugge = rug, a coarse, nappy, woollen cloth. 15 (Brathwait 1, lines 244, 254).

Salomon = Solomon; the reference may be to Proverbs 19. 17 or 22. 22. 15 (Brathwait 1, line 150).

scarfed = garments that hang loosely from the shoulders or dress. 8 (Hall).

scathe = damage, hurt. 9 (Munday 1).

sed Emporium laneis pannis celeberrimum = But a most famous market for woollen cloths. 2 (Leland).

sheereman = shearman, one who sheared the superfluous nap off the cloth, often a shearman-dyer, and sometimes an important middle-man. 14 (Deloney), 15 (Brathwait 1, lines 234, 238), 19 (Brathwait 3).

shrogs = underwoods. 9 (Munday 1).

sphere = In the old cosmogony the moon, the sun, the different planets and the so-called fixed stars were supposed to be set on concentric transparent spheres that revolved about the centre of the earth. Heaven was supposed to be located beyond the outermost sphere of the fixed stars. 15 (Brathwait 1, line 183).

staples = a place having the exclusive right of purchase of certain goods destined for export. 15 (Brathwait 1, line 207).

studdles = the upright posts of a loom. 15 (Brathwait 1, line 128).

Sturbidge = Stourbridge Common, to the East of Cambridge, where a famous fair was held. 15 (Brathwait 1, lines 374, 382, 385), 21 (Fuller).

swete = sweat. 3 (anonymous).

Taberer = taborer, one who beats the tabor, a small drum. 18 (anonymous).

tallow-catch = ? a dripping-pan. 7 (Shakespeare).

tenter = a frame for stretching cloth to set or dry. 15 (Brathwait 1, lines 228, 240).

the = thee. 3 (anonymous).

thorough = through. 11 (Tyrer).

tired = attired. 10 (Munday 2).

Tirus = the Biblical Tyre. 11 (Tyrer).

unde et = whence. 2 (Leland).

vent = sale. 12 (Camden 2).

waine-men = waggoners. 18 (anonymous).

white-coates = soldier wearing white or light-coloured coat; archers in the border wars. 15 (Brathwait 1, lines 529, 541, 544).

yuy = ivy (not yew). 1 (anonymous).

EDWARD MERYON WILSON

A note by his brother
Lord Wilson of High Wray
(Paul N. Wilson)

My brother Edward died in Cambridge on 21 November 1977 after a short illness, aged 71. Upon his last visit to Kendal he spent many hours with Mr. Bruce Jones, County Archivist of Cumbria and Miss Sheila MacPherson, his deputy discussing the final typescript of *Much Cry of Kendal Wool*, but did not live to see and check the galley proofs. This work has fallen largely on the shoulders of Miss MacPherson outside office hours. On my brother's behalf I would like to express my sincere thanks to her for undertaking this task.

Most readers of this book will know little or nothing of Edward Wilson. A few words about him and his background will not come amiss.

Our family has lived in Kendal for two hundred and fifty years and in or on the borders of the old county of Westmorland since the reign of Queen Elizabeth I. Edward took degrees in English and Modern Languages (Spanish) at Cambridge, won several scholarships, lectured in Spanish at Cambridge, and spent the war in the Ministry of Economic Warfare. He was appointed Cervantes Professor of Spanish at King's College, London, in 1945 and moved to become Professor of Spanish at Cambridge from 1953 to 1973. He was an acknowledged expert on the Spanish literature of the 16th and 17th centuries, and became very interested in bibliography and printing. He was a member of the Syndic of the Cambridge University Press.

As his work at Cambridge relaxed upon his retirement, he turned his attention to Kendal and Westmorland, and as his knowledge of English literature covered much the same period as that of Spain, he knew exactly how to go about finding the obscure references which are contained in this book.

His colleague Robert Coleman wrote of him in the *Emmanuel College Magazine* (Cambridge) that he had a most remarkable memory and if an argument arose in the Common Room as to who wrote what – within or even outside his period – Edward always came up with the correct answer.

Kendal and South Westmorland have produced some fine scholars: Bishop Watson and Sir Arthur Eddington are names which spring to mind. Edward Wilson was in the same class.

P.N.W.